The

SOAP BOOK

The

SOAP BOOK

SIMPLE HERBAL RECIPES

SANDY MAINE

The publisher gratefully acknowledges EsScentuals of Ft. Collins, Colorado, for the loan of photography props.

The Soap Book
Sandy Maine

Cover design, Susan Wasinger, Signorella Graphic Arts
Photography, Joe Coca, except as follows: Nancie Battaglia pages 15, 17, 21, 33, 37, and author photograph
Production, Marc McCoy Owens

 Interweave Press, Inc.
201 East Fourth Street
Loveland, Colorado 80537
USA

Printed in Hong Kong by Sing Cheong

Library of Congress Cataloging-in-Publication Data

Maine, Sandy, 1957–
    The soap book : simple herbal recipes / Sandy Maine.
        p.   cm.
    Includes bibliographical references and index.
    ISBN 1-883010-14-4
    1. Soap.   I. Title.
TP991.M26   1995
668'.124—dc   95-4865
                                               CIP

First Printing: 20M:695:CC
Second Printing: 10M:596:CC
Third Printing: 15M:896:CC
Fourth Printing: 10M:1096:CC

To my mother, Ruth Smithoover, and her well-tended grandsons, Eli and Clark-Cody Maine;

my husband and best friend, Louis Maine;

and the great circle of life.

TABLE OF CONTENTS

If you fall hopelessly in love with the splendid craft of soapmaking, you will not be alone! Although this craft was virtually unheard of fifteen years ago, it has quietly emerged as one of the most exciting new endeavors in the crafting world. Hundreds of converts are at their soap pots this very moment stirring, brewing, and sniffing!

If you love herbs, you will love soapmaking. If you love creating and concocting in your own kitchen, you will love soapmaking. If working with beautiful

essences, colors, and textures to perfect fragrant chunks of coveted handmade soap seems appealing . . . well, let me assure you *it is!*

As your soapmaking skills are perfected, you will find

There are countless varieties of soap you can concoct in your own kitchen.

yourself in great demand. New friends will appear. Old ones will appear more often. All of them will be after your soap!

My love affair with soapmaking began in my farm house kitchen fifteen years ago. Since that time it has taken over three buildings, flown me around the world, and landed me with fifteen wonderful employees who make, market, and ship my soap creations around the world. As this is being done, I am able to sit and share with you the romance of soapmaking.

Soap, loosely defined, is any substance that can be utilized with water to decrease surface tension in an effort to attract away some other unwanted substance.

Soap, even in its most archaic form, has probably always played a role in human history. Before soap became an intentionally produced product, it was extracted from plants like yucca, soapwort, and horsetail by our ancient ancestors. The need for a substance to aid in removal of dirt, grease, foodstuffs, pitches, bodily excretions, etc., has always been a part of the human experience. And so, I feel confident in saying that where there has always been a need, there has always been a response to that need.

The first known written mention of soap was on Sumerian clay tablets dating about 2500 B.C. They were found in the area of the Tigris and Euphrates rivers (in what is now known as Southern Iraq). The tablets

Soap, even in its most archaic form, has probably always played a role in human history.

spoke of the use of soap in washing wool. Another Sumerian tablet, dating 2200 B.C., describes a soap formula of water, alkali, and cassia oil.

The excavation of Pompeii, a city that was buried under the eruption of Vesuvius in A.D. 79, revealed the existence of an entire soap factory.

The Ebers Papyrus, a medical document from about 1500 B.C., shows evidence that Egyptians bathed regularly and that they combined animal and vegetable oils with alkaline salts to create a soap-like substance for washing.

Ancient Roman legend gives soap its name. From Mount Sapo, where animals were sacrificed, rain washed a mixture of melted animal fats and wood ashes down into the Tiber River below. There the soapy mixture was discovered to be useful for washing clothing, fur, and skin.

The Roman baths were built around 312 B.C. They were luxurious, popular, and in later years equipped with soap. It is believed that the Romans acquired the knowledge of soap from the Gauls. The Greek physician Galen, aware of the value of soap, recommended it for bathing and maintenance of health.

With the fall of the Roman Empire in A.D. 467, the popularity of soap and bathing went into decline. The resulting lack of cleanliness contributed heavily to the terrible plagues of the Middle Ages. Though many non-European cultures maintained bathing practices throughout the medieval period, it wasn't until several centuries later that bathing would come back into fashion in Europe.

Soapmakers' guilds began to spring up in Europe during the seventh century. No doubt, secrets of the trade were closely guarded. The training and promotion of craftsmen within the trade was highly regulated. The positions of apprentices, journeymen, and master soapmakers were much sought after. Italy, Spain, and France were early production centers for soap due to the excellent supply of oil from olive trees and barilla (a plant whose ashes were used to make lye).

Historical documentation shows that the English began soapcrafting during the twelfth century. King James I granted a monopoly to a soapmaker for $100,000 a year. The year was 1622!

For the next several centuries soap was heavily taxed as a luxury item, and so in European culture it was readily available only to the rich. It is said that Napoleon paid two francs for a bar of perfumed Brown Windsor.

In 1853, when the English soap tax was repealed, a boom in the soap trade and a change in the social attitudes toward personal cleanliness went hand in hand.

In Colonial America, soap was made by women and was part of a seasonal cycle of various home productions. The commercial production of soap did not commence until 1608 when several enterprising soapmakers from England arrived in the New World.

Scientific advancements that affected the soapmaking trade began with Nicholas Leblanc, a French chemist who in 1791 patented a process for making an alkali from common salt. The Leblanc process allowed for the inexpensive production of soda ash.

In the early 1800s, Michel Chevreul, another French chemist, made significant discoveries about the relationship of fats, glycerine, and fatty acids. His achievements laid the groundwork for the chemistry of soaps and fats.

During the mid-1800s, Belgian chemist Ernest Solvay discovered the ammonia process that improved the methods for extracting soda ash from common salt. His discoveries allowed for the increase in availability and quality of soda ash for soapmaking.

Sunfeather produces more than 140,000 pounds of soap per year.

These scientific advancements helped the soapmaking industry flourish in America by the mid-1800s. Soap became a popular and easy-to-obtain commodity. It also began to take on many different identities: soap for bathing, soap for clothing, soap for cleaning.

The marketplace was ready for variety, and the manufacturers complied. Companies such as Armour Soap Works (now the Dial corporation), J. S. Kirk and Company, N. K. Fairbank Company, and many others paved the way for the giant soap companies familiar today: Colgate-Palmolive, Proctor and Gamble, Dial, Jergens, and Lever Brothers. Cashmere Bouquet, Ivory, Lifebuoy, Woodbury, Lux, Camay, Zest, Tone, Safeguard, Caress, and others became mass-marketed common fare in the homes of most Americans.

In the mid-1970s a new era of deodorant soaps came into vogue with names like Irish Spring, Coast, and Shield. Following that came mass-marketed specialty soaps such as Neutrogena, Basis, and Oil of Olay.

Also at this time a woman named Ann Bramson published a short and simple little book that may well have begun a revolution in the soapmaking industry in America and abroad. The book was entitled *Soap: Making it, Enjoying it* (New York: Workman Publishing Co., 1972, 1975). Little did anyone know that Ann's book would spawn the revival of soapmaking as a home craft and a significant micro-industry in America and in other countries as well.

Consumers who are bored with mass-produced and mass-marketed products have welcomed the new era of small-scale soapcrafters to the marketplace. Should I attempt to name names? Here are a few: North Country Soaps, SunFeather Handcrafted Herbal Soap Company, Woodspirits, Shepards Mountain Herbal, Vermont Soaps, Adirondack Soap and Candle . . . the list goes on.

Together these small soap manufactories are enjoying at least 3 percent of the specialty soap market. At the same time their creativity and high-touch soap crafting is creating a love for the craft and the product, and a demand for more of the same.

Articles on home soapmaking began to appear in various publications in the mid-1980s. SunFeather Handcrafted Herbal Soap Company was the first company to offer soapmaking books, supplies, kits, and videos for the home soapmaker and/or the budding soap manufacturer. At the time of this printing at least 6000 home soapmakers/hobbyists and 150 micro soap sellers are known in the United States.

Interestingly, one may find

kindred soap folk sharing recipes and "cyber-sapo babble" (or should I say bubble?) on the Internet!

Yes, the history of soap when updated to 1995 includes a vigorous and growing interest and involvement among common, everyday folk.

Soapmaking has journeyed full circle through history from individual production to mass production and is now once again returning in a small yet significant way to individual production. I hope this book and the ones who read it exist as co-creators in the renaissance of the fine craft of soapmaking.

Sandy uses a press to cut a fresh batch of soap into bars.

CHEMISTRY, QUALITY, AND RAW MATERIALS

Chemically speaking, soaps are water-soluble sodium or potassium salts of fatty acids. Soap is created when fats and/or oils or their fatty acids are treated chemically with a strong alkali.

Fats and oils to be used in soapmaking can come from animal or plant sources. Each fat or oil is composed of its own unique mixture of several different triglycerides.

Fatty acids are the components of fats and oils that can be utilized for soapmaking. They are actually weak acids chemically composed of two parts: a carboxylic acid group and a hydrocarbon chain.

An alkali is a soluble salt of an alkali metal of sodium or potassium. Prior to the commercial production of alkali, they were produced from the ashes of plants. Chemi-

The quality of your soap creations will depend on the quality of your raw materials, your equipment, and your commitment to good and careful work.

cally, alkali is a base (the opposite of an acid). The base reacts with and neutralizes any acid that it comes in contact with. Alkalis used in soapmaking are sodium hydroxide (NaOH), also known as caustic soda, and potassium hydroxide (KOH), also called caustic potash.

The formulations used in this book will call for sodium hydroxide (lye). It is available in most grocery stores in the household cleaning supply section. It can also be purchased in small quantities via mail order. For larger quantities, seek out a chemical supply house.

Saponification is the chemical reaction that occurs when fats, oils, and caustics are put into contact with each other under controlled circumstances.

The soapmaking methods described in this book employ

what is known as the "kettle method" of soapmaking. This is the oldest and easiest method for the home soapmaker.

The mass production of soap is best accomplished with what is known as the "continuous method". But rest assured, the kettle method can be adapted for production should you wish to try your hand at it.

The quality of your soap creations will depend on the quality of your raw materials, your equipment, and your commitment to good and careful work. As you progress through the failures and successes in your soapmaking endeavors, you will come to understand quality and know when you have achieved it.

Quality soap looks good, smells great, and feels wonderful. Quality can be tested using pH test strips. Soap for use on skin should have a pH of 8 to 10. My own favorite testing method is the "touch-your-tongue-to-it" method. If your tongue senses a burn, then you can be certain that your soap has not completely saponified, that there is enough "free lye" within your soap to play havoc with your skin. Should you end up with a batch of poor quality soap, these mistakes are best put into a jar, covered with boiling water, and left to jelly. They can then be used 50/50 with your laundry detergent on washing day.

Let's talk about raw materials. If you can, it is best to get water from a rainstorm, a soft-water well, or a spring. The softer the water the better the soap. If soft water isn't available, you may use distilled or tap water. Oils and fats should smell and look fresh and clean. Essential or fragrance oils are usually of a high quality, and so you are responsible only for how they are blended and at what strength they are used.

All of the scent formulations in this book have been tried and found to be of beautiful and exquisite scent. But certainly some of you will not resist the temptation to blend and mix oils creatively on your own so that you may discover a scent that is altogether new.

Sandy pours soap into a well-greased mold.

AROMACRAFTING AND AROMATHERAPY
PRINCIPLES IN SOAPMAKING

In these fragrant times, aroma has come to mean many things to many different people. To the soapmaker, aromacrafting becomes an endeavor no less important than soapmaking itself.

You have many choices in aromacrafting. Perhaps you are willing to "play the field" with your raw materials, that is to say perhaps you are willing to use synthetic fragrance materials exclusively or in tandem with true essential oils. If so, your costs will be lower and your range of scenting options will be greater. When working with synthetic materials, I always try to keep in mind that they are still made

Good essential oils are the key to aromatic mastery.

from and inspired by our precious earth. I maintain an attitude of gratefulness toward them, though it seems that I can never experience perfection with them as I can with the true essentials. If you are an herbal purist, you will not settle for anything less than oils derived from pure plant sources.

If you are like most aromacrafters, you will probably find yourself in the middle of all of these options. You will enjoy working with a full range of true and synthetic scent choices as you employ them in myriad ways.

Aromacrafting is a term that I use for the amateur engaging in what is known as perfumery in the professional world .

Perfumers are an eclectic segment of culture. Some are highly and formally trained; others work off of natural talent. All are a creatively and monetarily inspired group . . . a special lot of

For me, aromacrafting begins with inspiration. A memory, a feeling, an appreciation for something beautiful— these become the nourishment for an inspired desire to create a scent.

people who bring more to your world than you may realize. I believe that these highly talented people deserve to be recognized for who they are and for what they are able to do. It would be unfair to consider yourself a perfumer when, in fact, you are a hobbyist aromacrafter.

For me, aromacrafting begins with inspiration. A memory, a feeling, an appreciation for something beautiful— these become the nourishment for an inspired desire to create a scent. From there the experience becomes an intuitive one where your dream mind searches for answers to the questions a scent poses. Days and weeks can be spent with a desire to create or recreate some special aroma. Your intuitive mind will work to answer the questions and then one day you will sit down to discover that your contemplations are over and the scent can be brought to life.

Impromptu aromacrafting occurs when you sit with many scent materials before you, and the creative blending process occurs rather quickly. It's almost as if the oils themselves become your inspiration and you become their creative channel for blending. Synergy occurs . . . and scent is born.

Aromatherapy is an interesting concept that has been in existence for thousands of years. Recently, it has enjoyed a resurgence in popular culture. This is evidenced by many new books and articles on the topic. It is also visible in new product development in the specialty skin care and bath industries.

Basically, aromatherapy is a practice by which true plant essences are administered to the receiver through the senses of smell, feel, and taste. The nose, skin, and mouth become gateways to the body and soul of the aroma recipient.

The opinion is widely held that plant oils have unique vibrations capable of affecting the physiological, mental, and spiritual well-being of individuals.

The theory that body, mind, and spirit are a unified whole and that the mental state of an individual affects his or her entire health is considered proven.

The goal, therefore, of aromatherapy is to harmonize the inner life-forces that may be out of balance.

Can we apply these principles to soapmaking? Of course we can! Soap is a fine and fairly stable place to store scent. Along with a warm bath or shower, or a plunge into a cool river for that matter, soap is a wonderful way to bring the various gifts of scent to your being.

Entire books on the topic of essential oils and aromatherapy have been written should you have an interest in gaining further knowledge re-

garding the specifics of this art. My favorite book (which is listed in Suggested Reading) is called *The Aromatherapy Handbook.* As an aromacrafter, you will surely wish to learn more about this fascinating subject.

Aromacrafting requires very little to begin: a half dozen small jars with lids (baby food jars are perfect), a pair of measuring spoons, clean rags, notebook and pencil, pressure-sensitive labels, and an indelible marking pen. Also, you will need a collection of essential and/or fragrance oils, two to four ounces of each. The more the merrier, of course. But if you are just beginning, you can work with as few as three or four varieties.

Most blended scents are composed while the artist remains mindful of three composition aspects of aromatic form.

1. Top notes are usually citrus or floral. They give the first impression in the blend.

2. Modifiers support the top notes but may subtly change them. Jasmine and rose are considered to be modifiers.

3. Base notes give the blend its foundation. Sandalwood, oakmoss, patchouli, musk, civet, and the like are good examples of base notes.

Now you are on your way! Begin by selecting and measuring out a small portion of oil with your measuring spoons. Be certain to keep meticulous written records of all your additions. After adding something, take a whiff and determine what to add next. When you get something wonderful, stop. You can always make a copy of a blend and then work on different versions. Also, keep in mind that oils added to soap can and sometimes do change. Part of the crafting process involves working on variations until you get the perfect expression in the finished soap.

I test oil blends in soap in a very economical way that I will share with you here. First, you will need to make a small insulated box. I made mine out of insulating foam board and duct tape. A quicker way would be to use a cardboard box covered with a wool blanket. You will also need some small paper cups and wooden or plastic stir sticks. Old chop sticks work well and can be reused.

Oil tests are done in conjunction with making a regular batch of soap. Simply pour 1/8 cup of unscented soap mixture into each paper cup and work quickly to add warm (body temperature) test oils. The amount of test oil will vary, but one-half to one teaspoon is a good place to begin. Let your nose be your guide and remember to record what you have done. I normally have everything premeasured and labeled and have stir sticks in place. It's very important to work quickly toward getting your tests into the insulated box. A quick drop in temperature can result in an unusable test. As soon as your test batches are complete, get moving on completing (adding oils and herbs to) your regular batch of soap.

The recipes that I've included in this book come with their own wonderful and unique scents. These scents have been crafted by either myself or by one of my two favorite perfumers and scent consultants, Ester Morera or Sue Ryn Hildenbrandt of Hill Woman Productions.

Aromatherapy can affect your physiological, mental, and spiritual well-being.

Gather the following tools and equipment:

- A good quality (accurate) scale that measures in ounces and pounds up to at least two pounds. Please refer to appendix for sources.

- One sturdy wide-mouth glass jar or beaker (easy to pour from), minimum two-quart capacity.

- Two wooden spoons, slotted if possible, which should be reserved exclusively for soapmaking.

- A one-gallon (or larger) stainless-steel or enamel kettle. (Never use aluminum! It will react with your soap mixture, ruining both soap and kettle.)

- A two-cup plastic or glass measuring cup.

Common household items are all that you will need.

- One stainless-steel wire whisk, the smaller the better.
- One photographic or lab-quality thermometer that you can depend upon for accuracy. This thermometer must measure between 80°F and 110°F.
- One pair of well-fitting rubber gloves.
- Safety glasses.
- One plastic food-storage container with a lid, shoebox size or a bit larger. (This will be your mold.)
- Two blankets.
- One jar of vinegar. (This is only needed if you accidentally splash lye onto your skin. The vinegar can be used as a wash to neutralize the lye.)

For best results, keep in mind the following:

Choose a well-lighted work area with a sink and countertops. You may want to lay newspaper on your counter for protection.

Plan to make your first batch of soap during an uninterrupted time.

Plan to make your first batch of soap during an uninterrupted time. Allow yourself approximately one and one half hours.

Have all the necessary ingredients at your disposal. All materials can be purchased through health food stores, grocery stores, or by mail order (see Sources).

Throughout the soap-making process, remember to handle lye with great care! Keep it out of the reach of children and pets. It is extremely caustic in dry or wet form and will burn skin, blind eyes, remove paints and finishes, and redesign linoleum floors. It has little effect on enamel, stainless-steel, glass, copper, plastic, rubber, or wood. It will play havoc with everything else. In the event of skin contact, flush with cool running water and douse with vinegar immediately. In the event of a spill, put your rubber gloves on and mop the spill with towels or rags.

Step 1

Put on your rubber gloves.

Weigh out 12 ounces of lye (sodium hydroxide) into the two-cup plastic or glass measuring container. Be certain to account for the weight of your measuring container.

Weigh 32 ounces (2 pounds) of *cold* water into the sturdy glass container. Again, be certain to account for the weight of your container.

Now it is time to mix the lye into the glass container of cold water. Put on your safety glasses. Because the lye will heat the water and fumes will be released, it is best to do this outside or under a ventilation fan. It is also wise to avert your face as much as possible to avoid inhaling the harsh and unpleasant fumes. (The fuming will only last for thirty seconds.)

Add the lye to the water slowly while stirring with a wooden spoon. As soon as all the lye is dissolved in the water, set it safely aside to cool.

Step 2

Weigh out 24 ounces of coconut oil and 38 ounces of vegetable shortening into the metal kettle. Remember to account for the weight of your container. Melt these oils over a low heat, stirring frequently. As soon as they have melted, remove them from the heat and add 24 ounces of olive oil.

Step 3

Keep your gloves on. This step involves getting the temperature of the lye to a range of 95°F to 98°F while at the same time getting the kettle of oils within the same temperature range. When both mixtures are within this range, combine them. Achieving this stage will require your full and careful attention.

Use hot or cold water baths to either raise or lower the temperatures of the mixtures. There is a knack to doing this skillfully, and it comes only with practice.

Now prepare your soap mold by greasing its sides and bottom with shortening.

Step 4

This is the fun part! Wearing rubber gloves and safety glasses, slowly pour a steady stream of the temperature-correct lye into the temperature-correct oils. Stir constantly in a relaxed circular motion until all of the lye has been added. By bringing the lye and oils into contact with each other, you are prompting a chemical reaction called saponification. Saponification is the creation of soap!

Step 5

Continue to stir for approximately ten minutes. Eventually you will notice a subtle change in the quality of your mixture. It will become slightly thicker and will seem more homogenized and creamy. These changes are very slight, but in time you will learn to recognize them. Ann Bramson, in her book about soapmaking, writes about tracing. Tracing occurs

Many dried botanicals will produce gratifying results.

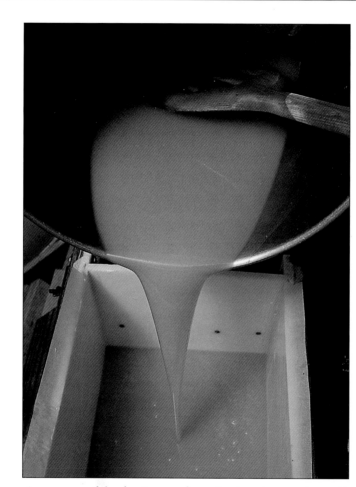

As soon as your oils have been incorporated, pour the mixture into your plastic mold.

when the soap mixture becomes thick enough to trace a design on the soap surface with dribbles of soap. This is the stage at which Ann recommends adding the scent oils and pouring the soap into its mold.

Personally, I prefer to catch the saponification process just prior to the tracing stage. At this earlier stage you can comfortably add scent oils and dried grains or botanicals without fear of the mixture becoming too thick.

Step 6

If grains, dried botanicals, or colorants are to be included in your soap, add them now. This is best accomplished by separating approximately two cups of unscented soap mixture and quickly whisking the dried goods into this small portion of soap until thoroughly mixed. Return this mixture to the soap kettle and stir.

Now is the time to stir in the scent oils—do not linger! If you delay, you will have a kettle filled with soap that cooled too quickly. As soon as your oils have been incorporated, it is time to fill your plastic mold (the shoe box sized plastic container).

Step 7

Put the lid over the warm and beautiful soap mixture. Set it in an undisturbed, warm place and cover well with many layers of blankets. (Wool seems to do the best job.) Allow the soap to sit undisturbed for eighteen hours to complete the saponification process.

Step 8

Remove the blankets and lid. You should now have a beautiful block of soap—firm, fresh, and fragrant. Allow it to sit uncovered for another eight to twelve hours before removing it from the box. To remove, simply turn the box upside down and allow the soap to fall onto a towel or a clean work surface.

If you have followed directions carefully, and if your scale and thermometer are accurate, you should have a beautiful batch of homemade soap.

If there are quality problems, you will notice a thin layer of oil on the top of your soap and a crusty chalk-like layer on the bottom. This malady is known as separation. If the separation is minor, you need only scrape off the top and bottom layers and discard them. The remaining soap should be fine. If gross separation has occurred, you will find more than a film of oil on top of your soap. It will look more like a pool of oil. In this case, you can be certain that your scale, thermometer, or mathematical methods were in error. Unfortunately, if this occurs you will need to discard the soap or use it for laundry purposes.

- Have your scent oils, dried botanicals, colorants or grains at approximately 98°F. This will prevent a quick loss in temperature when they are added to the soap mixture. The plastic mold should be at 98°F, too.

- Use shortening to grease the sides and bottom of your mold. Though optional, silicone bakery paper makes an excellent mold liner and will help prevent sticking. Lay it on top of the greased mold surfaces.

- Individual bar soap molds are fun to work with. If you are interested in trying them, I recommend greasing them well. Also be certain to get them into an insulated place as soon as possible because small volumes of soap can easily separate if allowed to cool too quickly.

Plastic molds in many shapes can be used for soap-making.

CUTTING, CURING, FORMING, PACKAGING, AND DECORATING

As soon as you are ready, you can cut your fresh soap into slices, bars, or chunks. You may also opt to leave it as it is and cut bars out of the large block as needed.

Should you wish to form or stamp it in any way, do this when the soap is still fresh and soft, within a few days. As time goes by and your soap begins to air dry (cure), it will become progressively harder and more difficult to cut. It never becomes too hard to cut, though this is done most easily within the first two weeks. This is because the water in the soap is constantly evaporating and diminishing. As the water evaporates, the soap will lose water weight and volume and can shrink as much as 10 percent.

A well-cured soap is exactly what you want. Not only will a well-cured soap last

You can cut your soap right away or leave it as it is and cut bars out of the large block as needed.

longer when subjected to the rigors of water, but it will also achieve its optimum mildness as it ages. Curing can best be accomplished by simply ex-posing your soap to warm dry air free from dust or dirt. Cure your soap for a minimum of two to three weeks before using.

Roll fresh soap into balls, or cut it into slices, bars, or chunks.

SOME FINISHING AND DECORATING IDEAS

- Roll fresh soap bars into balls. Do this by hand within a few days, while the soap is still fresh and soft.
- Carve soft bars into shapes or press designs and imprints into them.
- Paint designs on soap surfaces. Barbara West has written an entire book on this subject. (See Suggested Reading.)
- Make a soap-on-a-rope by forming soap around a knot at the bottom of a loop of cord any time after the soap has been taken out of the mold.
- Package your soaps in special paper or fabrics. Hand-painted watercolors and marbleized paper make lovely wrappers. Computer-generated graphics on the paper will give your soaps a professional look, and it's fun to decorate fabrics with ribbons, raffia, yarns, or string.
- Boxes, tins, and crates make wonderful gift sets.

Boxes, tins, and crates make wonderful gift presentations.

SPECIAL SOAPMAKING TECHNIQUES

CORATION

In former times, ochers, chromes, and metallic oxides of iron such as siennas and umbers were used with many mineral substances to color soap. By the late 1800s, colorants came primarily from aniline, a derivative of coal tar benzene, used as a base for extraction of color from other substances. Yellow and cadmium yellow came from naphthalene; red from vermilion; blue from ultramarine; green from borate of chrome; brown from chocolate modified with yellow or red.

Today, the home soapmaker has a vast assortment of coloring agents from which to choose. You may wish to achieve color only through natural means. Or you may find the wide array of waxed color chips (see Sources) more to your liking.

Waxed color chips are easy to use. Simply melt and mix them with a small portion of soap before adding to your kettle. This process should be done prior to adding any botanicals or natural colors. The amount of wax used will depend upon the hue you wish to obtain. One to four chips will be plenty for a batch of soap made from any of the recipes in this book.

NATURAL DYES

Again, the concentrations are up to you. All of the dyes listed below are available in powder form (see sources) except chocolate, which is available at supermarkets. I recommend melting bitter chocolate squares for brown. All dyes should be mixed with a small portion of soap prior to pouring into the kettle.

Chlorophyll = green
Turmeric = yellow
Ultramarine = blue
Ocher, Paprika = red
Chocolate = brown

MARBLING

To obtain a beautiful marbleized effect try this: Prepare two cups of unscented, colored soap mixture and set this aside while you scent the remaining soap in the kettle. Pour half of the scented soap into a plastic mold. Drizzle one cup of color in vertical and horizontal lines. Repeat with the remaining soap and color. To complete marbleizing, take a slotted spoon (or a chop stick for a different effect) and run it through the mold in a swirling direction, not more than twice. Cover the mold with the lid and blankets. Now you'll just have to wait!

LAYERING

Layering creates an attractive and unusual effect. In this process you put one layer of soap in the mold on day 1, another layer on day 2, and so forth. It is fun to try different combinations of color, texture, and scent. The best thing about layering is that it will give you an excuse to make soap everyday!

CHUNKING AND CHECKERING

You can create a confetti soap by chopping up small chunks of different colored soap and then adding these chunks to a newly poured batch. For this process to be successful, the newly poured batch should be as thick as possible.

If you'd like to try your hand at checkering, you'll need to make two or more batches of different colored soaps. Then, as soon as they are ready to cut, slice them into rectangular strips ap-proximately three quarters of an inch square. Lay these strips in your soap mold in a cross-hatch pattern. Now fill the mold with a fresh batch of soap of a different color.

BOTANICAL GLAZING

This technique of adding bits of dried herbs or flowers to the top of soap was invented by veteran soapmaker Barbara Bobo, owner of Woodspirits Soap Company, with inspiration from her friend Marianne Denniston of Seven Continents (see sources). Barbara was in the process of obtaining a design patent for this invention the last time I spoke with her. That means that this style of soap cannot be sold nor traded commercially without permission from Barbara. Thank you, Barbara and Marianne for sharing this technique with the home soapmakers of the world.

Make a batch of soap and cut it into bars of any size or shape. Allow them to cure for several weeks. These bars should be laid in a single layer in a flat plastic container, fitting them as close together as possible. Obtain clear glycerin soap from Pourette (see Sources) or simply purchase it from a store. Melt the glycerin soap in a double boiler and pour this over the tops of the pre-made soap bars. While the glaze is still soft, add dried potpourri or flowers. As soon as the glaze hardens, cut as closely to the soap bars as possible. The bars of soap will be covered on the top with a clear glaze which has dried flowers embedded into it. You may need to spend some time scraping away excess glaze, but the end result will be beautiful!

Add interest to your soap through coloration, marbling, layering, and glazing.

Love Light Soap

The Love Light Soap was inspired by the concept of universal love. Where there is love there is light.

The love light scent is composed of a blend of true essential oils. These oils offer scent vibrations that come from nature in a pure and perfect state of existance. I keep thinking that mere contact with these scents of perfection will offer a connection to your own perfection and capacity for creative expressions of love. This may be the soap to use if you need a little love light in your life.

Oil Blends
24 ounces olive oil
24 ounces coconut oil
38 ounces vegetable shortening (Crisco)

Alkaline Solution
12 ounces sodium hydroxide (lye)
32 ounces rain-, spring, distilled, or tap water

Essential or Fragrance Oil
1 1/2 ounces bergamot
1 1/4 ounces lemon
1 ounce patchouli
1/2 ounce bois de rose
3/4 ounce lavandin

Long before the phrase aroma therapy was popular, I was playing with and having great fun with patchouli soap. A warning label on every bar of patchouli soap stated, "East Indian patchouli oil is said to radiate a scent that charms. Sunfeather Patchouli Soap will leave you ready, willing, and charming!" Based upon the number of fan letters received and the volume of Patchouli Soap that has been made over the years, it has poven to be a charmer!

Oil Blends
24 ounces olive oil
24 ounces coconut oil
38 ounces vegetable shortening (Crisco)

Alkaline Solution
12 ounces sodium hydroxide (lye)
32 ounces rain-, spring, distilled, or tap water

Essential or Fragrance Oil
4 ounces patchouli

Fire Light

Fire Light is a favorite aromatherapy soap. It carries a deeply sweet, warm scent that aids in relaxation and the tapping of your creative abilities. Use this soap to kindle your sense of appreciation for and harmony with all that is. Allow it to aid in forming your dreams and wishes, and for manifesting your co-creative light. This is a soap for those who wish to nurture themselves and the world. Fire represents passion and action. Light represents clarity. Petitigrain, palmarosa, benzoin, orange, and patchouli combine to create a bathing experience you will come to cherish.

Oil Blends
24 ounces olive oil
24 ounces coconut oil
38 ounces vegetable shortening (Crisco)

Alkaline Solution
12 ounces sodium hydroxide (lye)
32 ounces rain-, spring, distilled, or tap water

Essential or Fragrance Oil
1 ounce benzoin
3/4 ounce palmarosa
3/4 ounce orange
1 ounce petitgrain
3/4 ounce patchouli

Sweetgrass has been revered for centuries by Native American people who used the smoke of this special plant for purification, protection, and upliftment. Traditionally, the smoke is engaged to carry prayers to the Creator.

The scent can only be described as heavenly. Because sweetgrass is rare and many people consider it a sacred plant, there is no commercial production of its essential oil that I know of.

Many years passed as I searched the world over for the perfect essential expression of this highly regarded plant. Somehow I knew that when my discovery was made, Sweetgrass Soap would become my absolute favorite.

In the fall of 1994, my search was rewarded and the first batch of Sunfeather Sweetgrass Soap was born. Gestation time: Eight years.

Oil Blends
24 ounces olive oil
24 ounces coconut oil
38 ounces vegetable shortening (Crisco)

Alkaline Solution
12 ounces sodium hydroxide (lye)
32 ounces rain-, spring, distilled, or tap water

Essential or Fragrance Oil
4 ounces sweetgrass (Available from Sunfeather. See Sources.)

Colorant
1 ounce chlorophyll powder or liquid

Bug Away Soap

This is an interesting aroma therapy soap. It is scented with a combination of basil, cedar, and eucalyptus oils. For me, its highest purpose is as an aid in repelling insects. Repelling insects is important when you live in the Adirondack Mountains, especially during black fly season, when you must actually face those pesky little biters just to get some warm sunshine on your face.

You can begin to take charge by using this soap. It will make your body scent confusing rather than attractive to the insects. Eventually, you will want to follow it with an application of Bug Away Oil mixed with olive oil or witch hazel.

Oil Blends
24 ounces olive oil
24 ounces coconut oil
38 ounces vegetable shortening (Crisco)

Alkaline Solution
12 ounces sodium hydroxide (lye)
32 ounces rain-, spring, distilled, or tap water

Essential or Fragrance Oil
2 ounces each basil, white cedar, and eucalyptus

Tigress soap is scented with oils that are useful for clearing the sinuses and for promoting circulation. The end result after a bath or shower with Tigress Soap is that your mind has been cleared, your body has been invigorated, and you are ready to unleash yourself on the world!

Juniper, lemon, and lime oil are easy to obtain through Frontier Herb Coop (see Sources). Camphor is available at most pharmacies.

My Grandmother used to keep a small bottle of smelling salts in her purse for mental emergencies. That was her tigress in a bottle!

If you need a tigress transfusion during the day, it is easy enough to keep a bar or sachet of Tigress Soap with you. If people look at you wonderingly for taking an aromatherapy sniff break, just give them a wiff.

Oil Blends
24 ounces olive oil
24 ounces coconut oil
38 ounces vegetable shortening (Crisco)

Alkaline Solution
12 ounces sodium hydroxide (lye)
32 ounces rain-, spring, distilled, or tap water

Essential or Fragrance Oil
$2\frac{1}{2}$ ounces juniper
1 ounce lemon peel
3/4 ounce lime
1/2 tablespoon camphor

Calendula Unscented Baby Soap

I have always loved growing calendula flowers and have often used them for making salves. When I tried using a calendula infusion in place of water for soapmaking, I was quite pleased with the results. Another method that I have found to be successful is to steep two cups of semi-dried calendula flowers in a sealed two-cup jar of olive oil for three weeks, strain the oil, and use it as a superfatting agent in soap. Calendula lends itself well to healing and nourishing the skin. I believe that this baby soap is the mildest, kindest soap available. It has been reported to cure, in short order, the diaper rash of baby Nicolas Lafountain while living with his mom and dad on a houseboat in Holland. They sent me a postcard just to say so!

Oil Blends
24 ounces olive oil
24 ounces coconut oil
38 ounces vegetable shortening (Crisco)

Alkaline Solution
12 ounces sodium hydroxide (lye)
32 ounces rain-, spring, distilled, or tap water

Essential or Fragrance Oil
4 ounces calendula and olive oil mix

T his soap was inspired by a problem patch of comfrey that had begun to overtake an entire section of my garden fifteen years ago. I was looking for a good use for the plant so that the plant's demise would not seem so cruel. I spent an entire day harvesting what seemed like a mile of comfrey root. I carefully washed and then dried the root on screens in the attic of my barn. The next task was to powder the root. Then I began experiments incorporating the root into soap formulas. Soon it became obvious to me that comfrey root powder turned soap into something splendid for sensitive skin. The green and mucilaginous comfrey plants give the soap a special healing, soothing quality as well as a beautiful dark violet color.

Collect and dry enough comfrey root to produce 4 ounces of powder (about one foot-long root). Roots must be thoroughly dry before pulverizing in a food processor.

Oil Blends
24 ounces olive oil
24 ounces coconut oil
38 ounces vegetable shortening (Crisco)

Alkaline Solution
12 ounces sodium hydroxide (lye)
32 ounces rain-, spring, distilled, or tap water

Essential or Fragrance Oil
2 ounces each lavender, rosemary, and aloe extract

Other
4 ounces comfrey root powder

Flower Fern and Moss Soap

I created this soap as a memorial to my favorite cat "Kid". He was an all-white cat with big green eyes and a formidable personality. Kid was very handsome and was quite proud of his beautiful white coat. He had a habit of coming home after his early morning rounds with the most beautiful scent on his fur. Of course he delighted in keeping the origin of this scent a secret from me. Eventually, I resorted to stalking him in hopes of discovering his "scentuous" secret. One early morning, with field glasses in hand, I spotted him rolling in a patch of oakmoss and wood ferns. That was all I needed, just a couple of simple clues with which to begin work on the Flower Fern and Moss Soap. If you enjoy a creamy soap, you may want to superfat with 2 ounces of warmed cocoa butter prior to pouring.

Oil Blends
24 ounces olive oil
24 ounces coconut oil
38 ounces vegetable shortening (Crisco)

Alkaline Solution
12 ounces sodium hydroxide (lye)
32 ounces rain-, spring, distilled, or tap water

Essential or Fragrance Oil
1 ounce patchouli
1 ounce lavender
1 ounce oakmoss

In the heat of the summer, peppermint soap is my first choice. It has a way of cooling the hottest skin and easing mild sunburns. When traveling long distances to craft markets, I always keep a "sniffing bar" of peppermint soap on the dash of my vehicle. No coffee needed!

The beauty of this soap is not only in its peppermint pungency and scintillating skin sensations—it also awakens and refreshes you in every way. With dried peppermint leaf added for color and texture, this soap is truly a gift from the garden.

Oil Blends
24 ounces olive oil
24 ounces coconut oil
38 ounces vegetable shortening (Crisco)

Alkaline Solution
12 ounces sodium hydroxide (lye)
32 ounces rain-, spring, distilled, or tap water

Essential or Fragrance Oil
4 ounces peppermint or a blend of peppermint and spearmint

Colorant
1/2 cup dried and crushed peppermint leaf

Lavender Soap

In response to my grandmother's gentle nudgings and long discourses on her favorite soap (lavender), I began experimenting with French and Spanish lavender oils early in my soapmaking career. I came to appreciate both. In the beginning I purchased 4-ounce bottles. Now it arrives in 55-gallon drums. The quality remains the same.

Lavender oil creates a soap that is stimulating and antiseptic to the skin. Lavender is very soothing to the senses. I have often recommended it to people with acne or overly oily skin. I have tried adding lavender leaf to this soap but without success. The creamy white bar and the pungency of lavender oil are a winning combination that rates highly with elderly women and others akin to lavender.

Oil Blends
24 ounces olive oil
24 ounces coconut oil
38 ounces vegetable shortening (Crisco)

Alkaline Solution
12 ounces sodium hydroxide (lye)
32 ounces rain-, spring, distilled, or tap water

Essential or Fragrance Oil
4 ounces lavender

Lemon Verbena Soap has been with me since the beginning of my soapmaking career. Having been an avid drinker of lemon verbena tea and an avid grower of the plant, it was a natural for me to create this soap for the Sunfeather line. I like to blend verbena oil with a small addition of lemongrass oil to aid in fixing the scent.

Oil Blends
24 ounces olive oil
24 ounces coconut oil
38 ounces vegetable shortening (Crisco)

Alkaline Solution
12 ounces sodium hydroxide (lye)
32 ounces rain-, spring, distilled, or tap water

Essential or Fragrance Oils
4 ounces lemon verbena

Colorant
1 ounce tumeric or yellow color chips (optional)

Little Cherub Chamomile and Lavender Baby Soap

My mother and I wrote the poem that follows when my third son, Clark Cody Maine, was one week old. The soap was born several weeks later. It has proven very effective against diaper rash and skin eruptions on the faces and bottoms of little cherubs.

Little cherub soft and pink,
Enjoys a bath in Mommy's sink.
Little one so soft and rosy,
Like the petals of a posy,
With chamomile and lavender, too,
Little cherub, our love is true.

Oil Blends
24 ounces olive oil
24 ounces coconut oil
38 ounces vegetable shortening (Crisco)

Alkaline Solution
12 ounces sodium hydroxide (lye)
32 ounces rain-, spring, distilled, or tap water

Essential or Fragrance Oil
1/2 ounce chamomile
3 ounces lavender

One morning in the early spring of 1991 I was helping Luke and Willy Daily boil sap in their steamy, fragrant sugarhouse way back in the woods. I was trying to take a few days off from work to celebrate this local rite of spring.

Maybe if Willy hadn't put a phone line out to the sugarhouse, I would have had my way.

But no! The phone rang and word came that Dayton-Hudson wanted a line of six new soaps. They wanted me to call them within the hour with plans. This was the hour that the Rosemary Morning Soap was born (somewhat against my will).

Rosemary is my ten-year-old neighbor. She was there. She was an inspiration. Her face smiles like a sunny morning.

Oil Blends
24 ounces olive oil
24 ounces coconut oil
38 ounces vegetable shortening (Crisco)

Alkaline Solution
12 ounces sodium hydroxide (lye)
32 ounces rain-, spring, distilled, or tap water

Essential or Fragrance Oil
4 ounces rosemary

Colorant
2 ounces each powdered dill weed and dried rosemary

Buffalo Restoration Soap

The Buffalo Restoration Soap is an example of how I have been able to work my own personal interests into my soapmaking.

I have been a buffalo lover since my South Dakota childhood. So, when discovering the Inter Tribal Bison Cooperative of Rapid City, South Dakota (an organization whose mission is to restore bison to Native Americans and their lands on the praries), I absolutely could not resist the temptation to celebrate my find with a new soap! I truly wanted to support this effort with a soap that would tithe money to the project. I'm quite certain that most of my workers and family had little faith in this very obscure market. But, that was only months before Dances with Wolves and Ted Turner's Bison Ranch turned nationwide attention toward the beloved bison. The rest of this story has yet to fully unfold. Let me just say that the Bison are making a comeback to the hearts (and tables) of people worldwide and sales for the Buffalo Restoration Soap are strong. I have chosen a traditional Native American scent blended from sage and cedar for this soap. The only buffalo in the soap is on the Sunfeather label.

Oil Blends
24 ounces olive oil
24 ounces coconut oil
38 ounces vegetable shortening (Crisco)

Alkaline Solution
12 ounces sodium hydroxide (lye)
32 ounces rain-, spring, distilled, or tap water

Essential or Fragrance Oil
2 ounces each sage and white cedar

Rosa Rugosa Pink Wild Rose Soap

This soap can be made only during the blooming time of the wild rose. It is one of the mildest soaps I've ever made, and the memory of making it is as good as any memory could ever be. You will remember your walk in the early morning sun. You will remember the bees and the scratches on your skin. You will remember the relentless picking of perfection and the scent of wild rose heaven. There will be a quiet memory of your walk home with a gallon pail full of roses . . . then the fragrant steam rising as you cover the roses with piping hot water. After the water cools, filter the rose water through a cloth and proceed to capture your summer morning in a batch of soap.

Oil Blends
24 ounces olive oil
24 ounces coconut oil
38 ounces vegetable shortening (Crisco)

Alkaline Solution
12 ounces sodium hydroxide (lye)
32 ounces rain-, spring, distilled, or tap water with fresh wild rose infusion

Essential or Fragrance Oil
4 ounces of your favorite rose oil

Colorant
As desired: melted pink crayon or red ochre or soap dye chips

Forest Garden Soap

Forest Garden was inspired by my husband's "garden" (a 90-acre family woodlot that was purchased in the 1940s for less than $20 per acre!) It's a beautiful, wild, and craggy place known as "the cobbles". Not unlike most gardens, it has been a place of hard work and reflective leisure. It has been thinned, planted, pruned and harvested—though the harvest is one of fuel rather than food.

I have come to appreciate this forest as my husband's garden. It's roots are his roots.

Forest Garden Soap is made with oils from the north woods. It reminds me of sleeping on balsam, washing with cedar tea, and weaving with white pine needles. It also has a cedarwood component that reminds me of my first batch of soap.

Oil Blends
24 ounces olive oil
24 ounces coconut oil
38 ounces vegetable shortening (Crisco)

Alkaline Solution
12 ounces sodium hydroxide (lye)
32 ounces rain-, spring, distilled, or tap water

Essential or Fragrance Oil
1/2 ounce balsam fir
$1\frac{1}{2}$ ounces cedar
$2\frac{1}{4}$ ounces vanilla
$1\frac{1}{2}$ ounces amber
$2\frac{1}{4}$ ounces musk (synthetic)
1/2 teaspoon cedarwood
1/2 teaspoon allspice
1/2 teaspoon patchouli
3/4 ounce frangipani
1/4 ounce oakmoss
3/4 ounce gardenia

I live in the beautiful northern region of the Adirondack Mountains. This soap was inspired by my desire to create a specialty soap that would catch the interest of the loggers, hunters, and outdoorsmen that are part of my local landscape. I wanted a soap that would sell down at the local store (and maybe in the L. L. Bean catalog, too).

Oil Blends
24 ounces olive oil
24 ounces coconut oil
38 ounces vegetable shortening (Crisco)

Alkaline Solution
12 ounces sodium hydroxide (lye)
32 ounces rain-, spring, distilled, or tap water

Essential or Fragrance Oil
4 ounces balsam fir

Oatmeal was the first filled soap that I made. It has a textural beauty that is hard to match. I find this soap a pleasure to make because it thickens so perfectly and cures much faster than other soaps. I love the simple, natural scent of the oat grains. Tradition-ally, oatmeal soap has been used for bathing children who have chicken pox or measles.

Oil Blends
24 ounces olive oil
24 ounces coconut oil
38 ounces vegetable shortening (Crisco)

Alkaline Solution
12 ounces sodium hydroxide (lye)
32 ounces rain-, spring, distilled, or tap water

Essential or Fragrance Oil
None

Filler
8 ounces powdered oatmeal (blenderized oats)

Woodspirits Botanical Glaze Soap

The technique for creating this soap is detailed in "Special Soapmaking Techniques" (page 42). The possibilities for creating beautiful soaps with this method are endless. I hope your experiments will be exciting and have splendid outcomes.

Top with glycerine soap glaze and sprinkle it with dried rose potpouri before the glaze hardens.

Oil Blends
24 ounces olive oil
24 ounces coconut oil
38 ounces vegetable shortening (Crisco)

Alkaline Solution
12 ounces sodium hydroxide (lye)
32 ounces rain-, spring, distilled, or tap water

Essential or Fragrance Oil
4 ounces rose oil

Colorant
4 ounces red ochre powder

There is a certain beauty to an unscented soap filled with tiny particles of bran and chaffs of wheat. Not only is it visually appealing, but the very subtle scents of the grains come through. I find these subtle and earthy scents calming to my soul. As far as tactile experience goes, you will find that a grain-filled soap which includes oatmeal, oat bran, and wheat bran to be soothing and healing to the skin.

Oil Blends
24 ounces olive oil
24 ounces coconut oil
38 ounces vegetable shortening (Crisco)

Alkaline Solution
12 ounces sodium hydroxide (lye)
32 ounces rain-, spring, distilled, or tap water

Filler
2 ounces pulverized oatmeal
2 ounces oat bran
1 ounce wheat bran
1 tablespoon whole oats (optional)

Gentleman Farmer Soap

As a child I would spend hours working soil from my grandmother's flower garden into various forms of mud pies. Grandmother was generous in allowing me to adorn my creations with her beautiful blooming flowers. At the day's end it was "Lava" soap (a hard working pumice handsoap) that grandma used to wash me with. A terribly harsh memory for five-year-old hands became the inspiration for a kinder hand cleaner later in life. Not only does the corn impart a beautiful color, but it also works effectively as an abrasive.

The technique is not hard to master. Simply blend two cups of soap mixture with cornmeal and whip with a wire whisk to remove all lumps. Return this mixture to the soap pot and add essential oils prior to pouring.

Oil Blends
24 ounces olive oil
24 ounces coconut oil
38 ounces vegetable shortening (Crisco)

Alkaline Solution
12 ounces sodium hydroxide (lye)
32 ounces rain-, spring, distilled, or tap water

Essential or Fragrance Oil
3 ounces lemon grass
1 ounce cedarwood

Filler
4 ounces ground cornmeal

Mr. Spicy Shaving Soap

One evening while I was having dinner at a friend's house, a creative surge came over me. One after another, names of soaps for men ran through my head. At first, I tried to ignore them, but they were so funny that I found myself smiling and unable to remain present with the company at hand. Finally, I excused myself to the study to jot down ideas until the creative surge exhausted itself. Sheepishly, I emerged from the study thirty minutes later with twelve new men's soaps for my line.

Mr. Spicy Shaving Soap has a high percentage of cinnamon oil, which stimulates and lifts the beard for a close and aromatic shave. This is a difficult soap to make because the cinnamon oil must be dribbled in quickly while stirring quickly. The cinnamon will streak the soap if you don't move deftly. You will also find that this soap thickens unusually fast. So be ready to pour immediately!

Oil Blends
24 ounces olive oil
24 ounces coconut oil
38 ounces vegetable shortening (Crisco)

Alkaline Solution
12 ounces sodium hydroxide (lye)
32 ounces rain-, spring, distilled, or tap water

Essential or Fragrance Oil
4 ounces cinnamon

Colorant
1 tablespoon cinnamon powder (optional)

Mechanics' Body Repair Soap

When I was carting hundreds of pounds of soap around to craft markets all over the Northeast, I became quite friendly with Obie, the local VW mechanic. He was able to keep my beautiful red VW van in perfect running condition and helped to ensure my safety on long and frequent road trips. The Mechanic's Body Repair Soap was inspired by Obie the mechanical craftsman and his talented hands.

This soap is filled with pumice and has the unusual ingredient of kerosene. Not only does kerosene give the soap a scent that only a mechanic would love, but it also acts as a degreaser. Couple the degreasing action with the abrasive nature of the pumice, and you've got a real body repair soap!

Oil Blends
24 ounces olive oil
24 ounces coconut oil
38 ounces vegetable shortening (Crisco)

Alkaline Solution
12 ounces sodium hydroxide (lye)
32 ounces rain-, spring, distilled, or tap water

Essential or Fragrance Oil
2 ounces Balsam fir
2 ounces kerosene

Filler
8 ounces pumice

In 1994 I received a flyer from Lynn Tolson of Kettlecare, Columbia Falls, Montana. I immediately became interested in her wonderful line of handmade salves and cremes. After sampling a few of her "wares", I invited her to collaborate on a couple of products. The Worker's Soap was created as a complementary product to her Worker's Salve. Now I market her salve and she markets my soap, and we are doing a good job of staying out of each other's way. The Worker's Soap has a blend of cornmeal and pumice. It has a spicy scent and seems to hold a special appeal for gardeners, artists, and others with working hands.

Oil Blends
24 ounces olive oil
24 ounces coconut oil
38 ounces vegetable shortening (Crisco)

Alkaline Solution
12 ounces sodium hydroxide (lye)
32 ounces rain-, spring, distilled, or tap water

Essential or Fragrance Oil
1 ounce cinnamon
2 ounces allspice

Filler
2 ounces each cornmeal and pumice

Driven by a well-loved addiction, I finally realized that chocolate soap's time had come. Though it has only been on the market for a few months, it is getting rave reviews! The only complaint: It doesn't taste very good! Oh, one other thing—I recommend that you have a chocolate bar handy near the shower or tub.

Oil Blends
24 ounces olive oil
24 ounces coconut oil
38 ounce vegetable shortening (Crisco)

Alkaline Solution
12 ounces sodium hydroxide (lye)
32 ounces rain-, spring, distilled, or tap water

Essential or Fragrance Oil
4 ounces chocolate fragrance
(I recommend my Sunfeather Chocolate Love-a-Lot fragrance oil blend, of course!)

Colorant
4 ounces cocoa powder (swirl technique)

Cocoa Butter Dry Skin Soap

This soap was my first attempt at the technique called superfatting. Superfatting occurs after you have created a chemical reaction in your soapmaking pot but before you have poured your mixture into a mold.

At this specific time in the soapmaking process just a few ounces of any warmed (not hot) specialty oil are added.

Superfatted soap is by far the creamiest and mildest of any soap. The secret lies in the fact that the specialty oil does not saponify with the other oils, but rather it remains in-dependent and performs as an emollient in the soap.

Cocoa Butter Dry Skin Soap is scented with a lovely blend of lavender and a touch of bitter almond. Only the most sensitive nose can discern the warm essence of the cocoa butter. But certainly, it is there.

Oil Blends
24 ounces olive oil
24 ounces coconut oil
38 ounces vegetable shortening (Crisco)

Alkaline Solution
12 ounces sodium hydroxide (lye)
32 ounces rain-, spring, distilled, or tap water

Essential or Fragrance Oil
1/2 teaspoon bitter almond
2 ounces lavender

Superfatting
2 ounces warmed cocoa butter

Though most of the fragrance materials in it are synthetic in composition, this soap has a strong, true vanilla scent. I make this soap with a fragrance oil that was created by Melissa Lettick, the Herb Lady of Harpers Ferry, West Virginia.

Oil Blends
24 ounces olive oil
24 ounces coconut oil
38 ounces vegetable shortening (Crisco)

Alkaline Solution
12 ounces sodium hydroxide (lye)
32 ounces rain-, spring, distilled, or tap water

Essential or Fragrance Oil
4 ounces vanilla fragrance (I recommend Mamma's Sweet Vanilla Oil, available from The Herb Lady)

Brown Windsor and Clay Soap

Brown Windsor Soap was historically documented to be Napoleon's favorite. So one day, I went about recreating it to see if men of the late 1900s would take a liking to it as well. I discovered that things have not changed much. The Brown Windsor scent still gets high marks among my male friends and soap testers. To add a sublime courseness, I like to include a measure of fine cosmetic-grade clay to this formula. It gives you something tactile to consider while your nose is wisking you back into the early nineteenth century.

Oil Blends
24 ounces olive oil
24 ounces coconut oil
38 ounces vegetable shortening (Crisco)

Alkaline Solution
12 ounces Sodium hydroxide (lye)
32 ounces rain-, spring, distilled, or tap water

Essential or Fragrance Oil
$3^{1}/_{2}$ ounces cassia
3/4 ounce cumin
3/4 ounce clove
3/4 ounce lavender
1/2 ounce thyme
3/4 ounce neroli petitgrain

Filler
8 ounces cosmetic-grade clay

Erotica's Bath Soap was created as a cooling compromise to a rather hot request for a private label soap. One morning I received a phone call from a mail-order marketer with a catalog called "Improper Taste". The owner was interested in having my company produce phallic soap on a rope and she wanted to order "a lot"!

Here I was, faced with my first moral soap dilema. Could I ask my workers to produce such a product? Did I want to listen to my small town respond to something so outrageous? Could I, in good conscience, use my business to promote an industry that I personally did not wish to support? Not wanting to lose a substantial account, I was determined to create a solution that would work for all concerned. So, I worked on designing a soap with an aromatherapy love scent and a tasteful yet "spicey" label. The Erotica's bath soap came into being and has been a "hot seller" ever since.

Oil Blends
24 ounces olive oil
24 ounces coconut oil
38 ounces vegetable shortening (Crisco)

Alkaline Solution
12 ounces sodium hydroxide (lye)
32 ounces rain-, spring, distilled, or tap water

Essential or Fragrance Oil
4 ounces patchouli
1/2 ounce bitter almond

SOURCES

Avena Botanicals
20 Mill St.
Rockland, ME 04841
Herbal products. Catalog, $2.

Chart Corporation, Inc.
787 E. 27th St.
Paterson, NJ 07504
(201) 345-5554
Botanical extracts.

Frontier Herb Cooperative
Box 299
Norway, IA 52318
(800) 669-3275
Essential and fragrance oils, unusual cold-pressed oils, herbs, clays and more.

Hill Woman Productions
44027 Cross Island Rd.
Wellesley Island, NY 13640
Fragranced and essential oil blends, herbal products. Send $.55 on a self-addressed envelope.

Pourette
6910 Roosevelt Way NE
Seattle, WA 98115
(206) 525-4488
Dyes, glycerine toppings, assorted molds.

SunFeather Handcrafted Herbal Soap
  Company
1551 Hwy. 72
Potsdam, NY 13676
(315) 265-3648,
  fax (315) 265-2902
Complete line of soapmaking supplies and kits, soaps, oils. Full-color 24-page catalog, $2.

Marianne Denniston
Seven Continents Mktg., Ltd.
PO Box 85
Pond Ridge, NY 10576
(914) 764-1958

Whittaker, Clark & Daniels, Inc.
100 Coolidge St.
South Plainfield, NJ 07080
(800) 732-0562
Minerals, colors, chemicals.

Barbara Bobo, Woodspirits
1920 Apple Road
St. Paris, OH 43072
(513) 663-4327

SUGGESTED READING

Bramson, Ann. *Soap: Making It, Enjoying It.* New York: Workman Publishing Co., 1972, 1975.

Cavitch, Susan Miller. *The Natural Soap Book.* Pownal, VT: Storey Communications, 1995.

Fisscher-Rizzi, Suzanne. *Complete Aroma Therapy Handbook: Essential Oils for Radiant Health.* New York, NY: Sterling Publishing Co., 1990.

Mohr, Merlyn. *The Art Of Soap Making.* Buffalo, NY: Camden House Publishing, 1979.

West, Barbara: *A Cowbody Christmas.* St. Louis, MO: Easíl Publications, 1993.

White, Elaine. *Soap Recipes.* Starkville, MS: Valley Hills Press, 1995.

INDEX